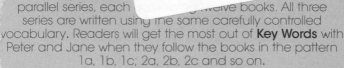

How do I

Key Words wit ~~parallel series, each~~ twelve books. All three series are written using the same carefully controlled vocabulary. Readers will get the most out of **Key Words** with Peter and Jane when they follow the books in the pattern 1a, 1b, 1c; 2a, 2b, 2c and so on.

• Series a
gradually introduces and repeats new words.

• Series b
provides further practice of these same words, but in a different context and with different illustrations.

• Series c
uses familiar words to teach **phonics** in a methodical way, enabling children to read increasingly difficult words. It also provides a link to writing.

Published by Ladybird Books Ltd
A Penguin Company
Penguin Books Ltd., 80 Strand, London WC2R 0RL, UK
Penguin Books Australia Ltd., Camberwell, Victoria, Australia
Penguin Group (NZ) 67 Apollo Drive, Rosedale, North Shore 0632, New Zealand

1 3 5 7 9 10 8 6 4 2

© LADYBIRD BOOKS LTD MCMLXIV, this edition MMIX

ISBN: 978-1-40930-131-8

Printed in China

Key Words

with Peter and Jane

8c

Fun with sounds

written by W. Murray
illustrated by M. Aitchison and J.H. Wingfield

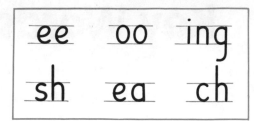

*

The boy uses sounds to help him make words.

He makes the words –

see	**bee**
book	**cook**
ring	**king**
shop	**fish**
sea	**tea**
each	**reach**

*Sounds we know from Book 7c.

See notes on back inside cover.

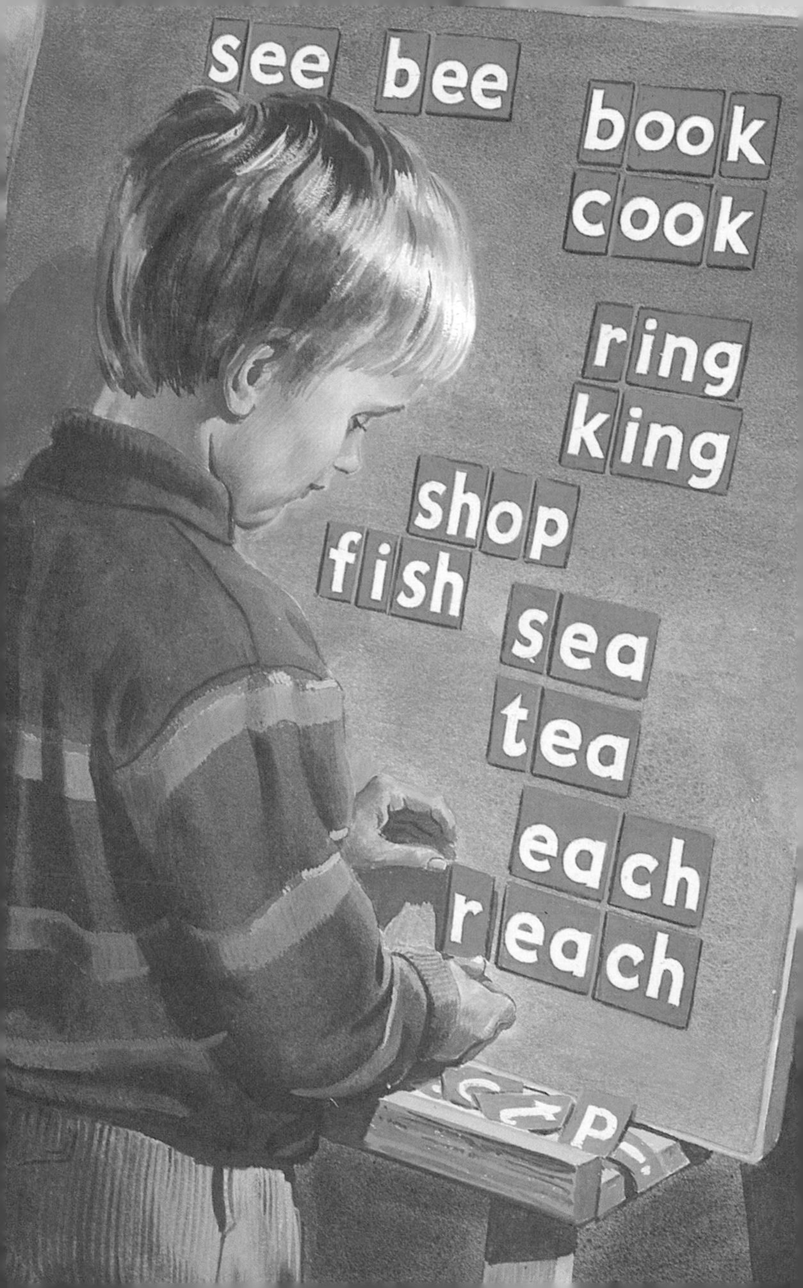
see bee
book
cook
ring
king
shop
fish
sea
tea
each
reach

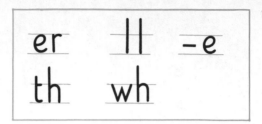

*

The girl likes to make words with the help of sounds.

She makes the words —

farmer	**fisherman**
bell	**hill**
pip	**pipe**
pin	**pine**
thin	**teeth**
whip	**which**

*Sounds we know from Book 7c.

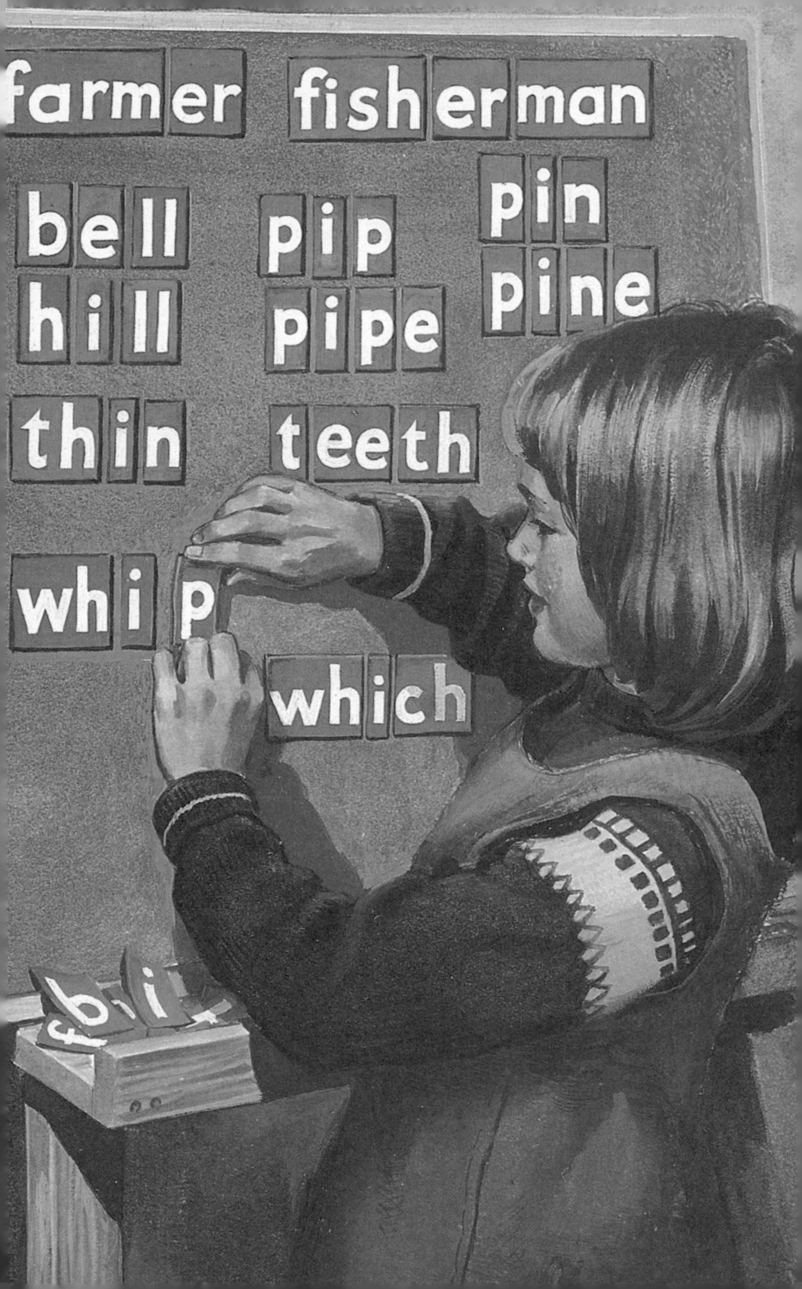
farmer fisherman
pin
bell pip
pine
hill pipe
thin teeth
whip
which

ai

We know the words: **rain, train** and **again.**

We can learn the words: **rail, sail, bait, wait, chain.**

The man has come to fish. He has his boy and girl with him. They have come by train. The boy and girl like to go by rail.

It has been raining, but it is sunny now. "I hope it won't rain again," says the man.

He baits his hook. Then he puts the hook with the bait into the water and waits.

The boy and girl watch. The girl has some flowers. She makes a chain of flowers as she waits. The boy has a boat which he wants to sail.

ay

We know the words: **day, may, play, say** and **away.**

We can learn the words: **stay, hay, pay.**

The children watch their father fish. Then they say, "We don't want to watch all day. May we play now?"

"Yes," says their father, "but please don't stay here. Go some way away as I want to go on fishing."

They go away and the boy sails his boat. Then he and his sister play in some hay that they find. They play hide and seek in the hay.

Then their father comes to say, "It is time to go home."

The boy looks at the fish. "Five fish and nothing to pay," he says.

oa

We know the words: **boat** and **road**.

We can learn the words: **moat, goat, coat, oak, load, foal, coal.**

The children are by a moat. The girls look at the ducks on the water. One of the boys puts his coat on a goat they are playing with.

A farmer goes by on the road with a load of hay. He sees the children and calls to them, "Stay away from the moat."

A man is by an oak tree with a foal. The girls go over to look at it. "It's a beautiful foal," says one girl.

"It's so black," says the other. "It's as black as coal."

st

We know the words: **stop** and **first.**

We can learn the words: **rest, post, stamps, cost, stick, stands, steps.**

The boy and girl are on holiday at a farm. Today their mother and father stay in the farmhouse for a rest, and the children go to post some cards and letters to their friends.

They know how much the stamps cost and they have money for them. First they buy the stamps and then they stick them on the letters and cards.

The farm dog is with them. He stands by the steps as they post the letters and cards.

Then they go back to the farm for their tea.

Complete the words as you write
them in your exercise book. The
pictures will help you.

ai   ay   oa   st

1 ch--n   2 h--

3 st--t   4 ne--

5 --amp   6 tr--n

7 tr--   8 t--d

The answers are on Page 48.

nd

We know the words: **and, hand, sand, stand** and **end.**

We can learn the words: **band, land, pond, mend, bend, wind.**

1 Here is a band.

2 The farmer looks at his land.

3 One boy sits and the other two stand.

4 The foal is by a pond.

5 She is going to mend her coat.

6 The trees bend in the wind.

OW

We know the words: **cow, how, now, down** and **flower.**

We can learn the words: **owl, fowls, tower, shower, town, clown.**

1 The owl looks down from the tree.

2 He helps the farmer with the fowls.

3 There is a tower on the hill.

4 They get wet in a shower of rain.

5 The man is in the town.

6 The children look at the clown.

aw

We know the words: **saw** and **draw**.

We can learn the words: **paw, raw, claws, straw, lawn, yawns.**

1   The cat puts its paw in a dish.

2   The meat is raw. She is going to cook it.

3   The bird has big claws.

4   The farm dog is on some straw.

5   The children play on the lawn.

6   The boy yawns. He wants to go to bed.

-ce

We know the words: **ice** (in ice-cream) and **nice.**

We can learn the words: **dice, mice, rice, race, face, place.**

1   Here are some dice.

2   This boy likes mice.

3   Mother uses some rice.

4   The children like to race.

5   She looks at her face.

6   She puts the tin in its place.

Complete the words as you write
them in your exercise book. The
pictures will help you.

nd ow aw -ce

1 be--

2 dr--in

3 --l

4 ra--

5 cl--s

6 ba--

7 t--el

8 di--

The answers are on Page 48.

ck

We know the words: **back, black, chick, duck, pick, thick** and **o'clock.**

We can learn the words: **peck, licks, kicks, lock, rock, socks, deck, sack.**

1   The fowls peck as they eat.

2   The girl licks the ice-cream.

3   The boy kicks the ball.

4   He opens the lock with a key.

5   A bird is on the rock.

6   The boy puts on his socks.

7   A man is on deck.

8   This man has a sack.

1

2

3

4

5

6

7

8

ar

We know the words: **car, jar, barn, park, card** and **garden.**

We can learn the words: **arm, star, bark, dark, park, mark, market, sharp.**

1 She takes his arm.

2 He draws a star.

3 The boy makes the dog bark.

4 It is dark in the barn.

5 They play in the park.

6 She makes a mark on the wall.

7 Here is a market.

8 This is sharp.

Some old fishermen sit on the sea wall and watch the boats. They do not go out to sea any more as they are too old. They talk to each other about old times and what they think the weather will be.

Another one mends a fishing net. Another is mending a little boat as he talks to a boy and girl. He tells them about his days at sea. He says that once he was on the deck when a whale hit his boat. "Over she went," he says, "and I had to swim to another boat."

Copy out and complete –

1 The old fishermen sit a-- watch the b--ts.
2 They are on the s-- wall.
3 One tells them about his d--s at sea.
4 On-- a whale hit his boat, he says.
5 He was on de-- when his boat was hit.

The answers are on Page 48.

A farmer buys a big black and white bull at the market. He brings him to his farm and puts him with his cows.

The next day a man on the farm goes to work by the cows. All at once the bull sees him. He does not like the look of the man and comes over to him. The man starts to run and the bull runs after him.

The man runs fast but the bull runs fast, too. The man is in danger. The bull may catch him. Then the man jumps over the gate just in time.

Copy out and complete –

1 A f - - mer buys a big bull.
2 The bull is bla - - and white.
3 The bull is with the c - - s.
4 The man st - - ts to run.
5 The bull runs fa - - .

The answers are on Page 49.

It is night time. There is a fox by the farmhouse. The fox wants to eat. He would like a fowl, or a duck or a goose. There are lots of these on the farm.

The farmer is in bed. He does not know the fox is about, but soon he hears his dog bark. Then he hears the fowls and the ducks. He jumps from his bed and runs out of the farmhouse. Then he sees the fox. When the fox sees both the farmer and his dog, he runs away.

Copy out and complete –

1 The fox wants to --t.
2 The farmer h--rs the dog b--k.
3 He runs d--n to see what is going on.
4 He s--s the fox.
5 The fox runs aw--.

The answers are on Page 49.

There is a nest in the tree and there are some little birds in it. One of them falls out of the nest on to the lawn. It cannot fly.

A cat is on the lawn. The cat likes to catch birds. He sees the little bird fall out of the nest and goes over to it.

A boy comes into the garden and sees the little bird and the cat. He takes the cat into the house. Then he picks up the little bird in his hand. It is soon in its nest again.

Copy out and complete –

1   A ne-- is in the tree.
2   A cat is on the l--n.
3   The cat likes to cat-- birds.
4   He pi--s up the bird in his ha--.
5   The bird is soon in its nest ag--n.

The answers are on Page 49.

One sunny summer day, two boys find a goat by a barn. There is a chain on the goat. The other end of the chain is round a post.

One boy says, "What a nice goat. I know another goat and he lets me play with him." He goes up to this goat with his hand out. But this goat does not like children. He runs at the boy and hits him hard with his head. The boy sits down hard. The other boy helps him up and they both run away.

Copy out and complete –

1 It is a sunny summer d--.
2 There is a ch--n on the g--t.
3 The chain is round a po--.
4 The boy says, "What a ni-- goat."
5 He says, "Another goat lets me pl-- with him."

The answers are on Page 50.

One of these boys has made a Go-Kart with the help of his father. They had a picture of a Go-Kart from a shop and got some help from this as they made their own Go-Kart.

The boy's father does not let him use the Go-Kart on the roads as there would be too much danger there.

The boy and his friend come down this hill fast. They have put some hay by the wall so that the Go-Kart cannot hit the wall on the way down. Both the boys have a lot of fun in this way.

Copy out and complete –

1   The boy a-- his father have made a Go-Kart.

2   The boy does not use the Go-Kart on the r--ds.

3   There is some h-- by the wall.

4   The boy and his friend come down the hi--.

5   They come down the hill fa--.

The answers are on Page 50.

The weather is bad. It has been raining for a long time. "Let's go and play in the barn," says one boy to the other. "There is more room there."

"Yes," says his friend, "we can play games there that we cannot play in the house."

The two boys go to the barn with their sisters. First they play cricket with a bat they have made. Then they play hide and seek in the straw.

One of the boys finds some sacks. They each get in a sack and then they have a sack race.

Copy out and complete –

1   There has been a lot of r - - n.
2   They go in the b - - n.
3   They play in the str - - .
4   One boy finds some sa - - s.
5   They have a sack ra - - .

The answers are on Page 50.

The children have their pets on the lawn. The little boy plays with his puppy and his sister gives her rabbit something to eat. The big girl is going to brush her kitten. Her brother has some mice in a big box.

"I like to look after my rabbit," says the little girl.

"It's fun to play with my puppy," says the little boy.

"Some people don't like mice," says the big boy, "but I like them very much. When I'm a man I hope to work at the Zoo."

The big girl says, "A pet is something to love."

Copy out and complete –

1   The children are on the l - - n.
2   The little girl l - - ks after her rabbit.
3   She gives it something to - - t.
4   The big girl is going to bru - - her kitten.
5   The big boy has some mi - - .

The answers are on Page 51.

Pages 48 to 51 give the answers to the written exercises in this book.

Page 16

1	chain	2	hay
3	stoat	4	nest
5	stamp	6	train
7	tray	8	toad

Page 26

1	bend	2	drawing
3	owl	4	race
5	claws	6	band
7	towel	8	dice

Page 32

1 The old fishermen sit and watch the boats.

2 They are on the sea wall.

3 One tells them about his days at sea.

4 Once a whale hit his boat, he says.

5 He was on deck when his boat was hit.

Page 34

1 A farmer buys a big bull.

2 The bull is black and white.

3 The bull is with the cows.

4 The man starts to run.

5 The bull runs fast.

Page 36

1 The fox wants to eat.

2 The farmer hears the dog bark.

3 He runs down to see what is going on.

4 He sees the fox.

5 The fox runs away.

Page 38

1 A nest is in the tree.

2 A cat is on the lawn.

3 The cat likes to catch birds.

4 He picks up the bird in his hand.

5 The bird is soon in its nest again.

Page 40

1 It is a sunny summer day.

2 There is a chain on the goat.

3 The chain is round a post.

4 The boy says, "What a nice goat."

5 He says, "Another goat lets me play
with him."

Page 42

1 The boy and his father have made a
Go-Kart.

2 The boy does not use the Go-Kart on
the roads.

3 There is some hay by the wall.

4 The boy and his friend come down the hill.

5 They come down the hill fast.

Page 44

1 There has been a lot of rain.

2 They go in the barn.

3 They play in the straw.

4 One boy finds some sacks.

5 They have a sack race.

Page 46

1   The children are on the lawn.

2   The little girl looks after her rabbit.

3   She gives it something to eat.

4   The big girl is going to brush her kitten.

5   The big boy has some mice.

Revision of sounds learned in this book

ai   ay   oa   st

nd   ow   aw   -ce

ck   ar

Learning by sounds

If children learn the sounds of letters and how to blend them with the other letter sounds (eg. c-a-t) they can tackle new words independently (eg. P-a-t).

In the initial stages it is best if these phonic words are already known to the learner.

However, not all English words can be learned in this way as the English language is not purely phonetic (eg. t-h-e).

In general a 'mixed' approach to reading is recommended. Some words are learned by blending the sounds of their letters and others by look-and-say, whole word or sentence methods.

This book provides the link with writing for the words in Readers 8a and 8b.